# THE Frango COOKBOOK

## Simple Recipes & Sweet Ideas

RECIPES BY
**Elizabeth Brown**

TEXT BY
**Steve Siegelman**

PHOTOGRAPHY BY
**Maren Caruso**

**BOOK
KITCHEN**
San Francisco

# Contents

# Introduction

For millions of Americans, there are chocolates, and then there are Frango Chocolates. And for every fan, there's a Frango personality. Some bite a single chocolate in half, letting it melt slowly on their tongue, their eyes half closed in dreamy bliss. Others pop one in their mouth and chew contentedly as a big, broad grin lights up their face. Most remain fiercely loyal to the original mint flavor, while there are those who love them all, from Dark Mint to Double Chocolate. But whoever they are, whatever their style, there's one thing all Frango fanatics have in common: they love the *tradition* of Frangos as much as the chocolates themselves.

Maybe it's because Frango Mints bring back childhood memories of family excursions to Marshall Field's, a holiday lunch at the Walnut Room, or a favorite midwestern relative who always brought them as a gift. Or maybe it's the experience of buying chocolates in a pretty box at a gleaming department-store counter. Frangos are fun. They make people happy.

And that's what this little book is all about. It's based on the simple idea that there's more to Frangos than just eating them straight out of the box. You see, because they're filled with wonderful flavor and made with premium ingredients, Frango Chocolates give you a head start in making all kinds of desserts, confections, and gifts. In these pages, you'll find dozens of recipes for turning Frangos into cookies, cakes, and special surprises. They're all easy and fun to make, and, thanks to the Frangos, their flavor will amaze you.

If you think Frango Chocolates make people happy, wait till you see what happens when you transform them into homemade treats. Start with a beloved American classic and add a little love of your own. With a sweet idea like that, you just can't go wrong.

# The Frango Story

Frango has been an American tradition for nearly a century, and today, that tradition is bigger than ever. It all started with a dessert—one that actually had nothing to do with either chocolate or mint. Maple Frango was a frozen confection with a flaky texture, served at the tearoom of the Frederick & Nelson department store in Seattle. Its name may have been concocted from "Frederick" and "tango," the dance craze that was sweeping the country at the time. Pies and fountain drinks were eventually added to the Frango line, and in 1927, the company's renowned candy maker, Ray Alden, created a chocolate mint Frango truffle. It would become one of the world's most famous candies.

When Marshall Field's bought Frederick & Nelson in 1929, the secret recipe for the Frango truffle was a major part of the deal. As soon as the purchase went through, Frederick & Nelson's candy makers were brought in to Field's flagship State Street store in Chicago to train the staff of the candy kitchen in the art of truffle making. The mints became an instant Chicago favorite.

For much of the twentieth century, that candy kitchen was the center of the Frango Mint universe. While most department stores smelled of perfume and cologne, the aroma of mint and melting chocolate filled the air and permeated the walls at Field's on State Street, beckoning customers to see, smell, and indulge.

Candy-kitchen confectioners would melt dark and milk chocolate in giant kettles and stir in a secret blend of flavorings and other ingredients. The mixture was poured out onto marble slabs to cool and then cut into individual pieces, which were passed under a curtain of pure melted chocolate in the enrobing machine. Once cooled, the chocolates were nestled in paper cups and packed by hand in signature green boxes.

In 1999, to meet worldwide demand for Frango Chocolates, the State Street candy kitchen was moved off-site to a larger

facility, where the candies are still made using the same secret recipe. Technological advances have made all kinds of new offerings possible, such as the limited-edition Frango Pink Mints created to raise funds for The Breast Cancer Research Foundation.

Today, more than a million pounds of Frango Chocolates are produced every year. New flavors, from Dark Mint to Double Chocolate, Caramel, and Hazelnut, have been embraced by legions of Frango fans all over the world, but the original Mint Chocolate remains by far the number-one seller.

In 2006, Marshall Field's became part of the nationwide family of Macy's stores. While the Field's name may be gone, the flavor and the magic of Frango live on. And at Macy's on State Street, the unmistakable aroma of melting chocolate once again wafts through the building. Just follow your nose to the Frango Café on the seventh floor, where you can see, smell, and sink your teeth into freshly dipped Frango treats made just for you.

## Frango Facts

The Frango Mint Chocolate is the best-selling flavor, with Double Chocolate running a distant second.

The Frango Mint Chocolate recipe calls for three kinds of chocolate.

Two hundred pounds of chocolate are melted to make each batch of Frango candy.

More than a million pounds of Frango Chocolates are sold each year.

Seasonal flavors have included everything from Candy Cane in winter to Passion Fruit in summer.

In 2005, Pink Frango Mints were created to benefit breast cancer research.

Other limited-edition offerings have included a Malt Shoppe Assortment and a Pie Assortment, with Apple, Pumpkin, and French Silk pie-flavored Frango Chocolates.

On November 14, 2002, Frango made big news when Marshall Field's created a 15-by-7-foot candy box, which was displayed at the Field Museum in Chicago. It held 90,090 Frango Chocolates and weighed in at 3,226 pounds, winning a spot in Guinness World Records™ for the Largest Box of Chocolates.

# Tips & Techniques

### STORING
Store Frango Chocolates as you would red wine: at cool room temperature in a dry, dark place. If the weather is very hot, you can refrigerate them, though this can cause "bloom," a cloudy white film on the surface. While unattractive, it is harmless and doesn't affect flavor.

For long-term storage, freeze Frango Chocolates. Wrap the box in plastic wrap or slip it into a resealable freezer bag for extra protection. To help prevent bloom, chill the chocolates gradually by putting them in the refrigerator for a few hours before transferring them to the freezer. Use the same two-step method for thawing: first put frozen Frango Chocolates in the refrigerator for a few hours, then move them to a dry, dark place.

### MEASURING
To keep things simple, all the recipes in this book call for Frango Chocolates by number of individual chocolates, rather than by weight or cup measure. There are 45 Frangos in a 1-pound box. If you prefer to work by weight, 3 Frangos weigh about 1 ounce.

### CHOPPING
Chop Frango Chocolates on a large cutting board, using a sharp chef's knife or a large serrated knife. Don't use a food processor, because the blade tends to heat the chocolates and melt them. When gathering up pieces of chopped chocolate, use the blade of the knife or a pastry scraper, rather than your hands, to prevent melting.

## MELTING

Many of the recipes in this book call for melted Frangos. Here are two easy methods. For both, be careful not to overheat the chocolates, which can cause them to burn or to seize and become grainy. You want to apply just enough heat to melt them, so always err on the side of underheating, then stir and continue to heat as needed. If the chocolate does overheat, you may be able to smooth it out by stirring in a tablespoon of solid vegetable shortening. Whenever you are melting Frangos for a recipe, stir until completely smooth before using.

**Microwave method:** Remove the chocolates from their paper wrappers and put them in a microwave-safe bowl. Heat the chocolates in the microwave oven at *half power* for about 2 minutes, let stand briefly, then stir. Microwave for additional 15-second increments as needed, stirring after each increment, just until the chocolate is melted. Using the microwave on full power may cause the chocolates to burn or seize or become too hot to handle safely. All microwave ovens are different, so start with a shorter heating period the first time you try this method. The chocolates may hold their external shape and not appear melted, so stir them well after each heating because their centers melt first.

**Double boiler method:** Remove the chocolates from their paper wrappers and put them in the top pan or bowl of a double boiler set over barely simmering water in the bottom pan. Or use a heatproof bowl that fits snugly in the rim of a saucepan. Make sure the water does not come into contact with the bottom of the top pan or bowl. Stir the chocolate occasionally, and remove it from the heat as soon as it is melted. Avoid heating the chocolate any longer than necessary, and don't let water splash into it, which can cause it to seize.

**TOASTING NUTS**

To toast nuts such as almonds, hazelnuts, pecans, pistachios, or walnuts, position a rack in the center of the oven and preheat to 350°F. Line a baking sheet with parchment paper, and spread the nuts on the baking sheet in a single layer. Toast, shaking the pan once or twice, for 7 to 10 minutes, or until the nuts are lightly browned and fragrant. To skin toasted hazelnuts, wrap the hot nuts in a clean dish towel and let cool for 10 minutes, then rub the nuts in the towel to remove their papery skins.

## Frango Flavors

Here's a list of the Frango flavors called for in this book. Many other flavors and products are available. For ordering information, see Resources on page 85.

**Frango Mint Chocolates**—The original classic: milk chocolate with mint–milk chocolate centers

**Frango Dark Mint Chocolates**—Dark chocolate with mint–dark chocolate centers

**Frango Double Chocolates**—Milk chocolate with milk chocolate centers

**Frango Dark Chocolate**—Dark chocolate with dark chocolate centers

**Frango Caramel Chocolates**—Milk chocolate with soft caramel centers

**Frango Chocolate Melts**—Melting disks, ideal for chocolate fountains and fondue; available in Double Chocolate and Dark Chocolate

**Frango Dessert Topping**—Available in Mint Chocolate, Double Chocolate, and Caramel

# Cookies & Confections

# Frango-Filled Shortbread Cookies

MAKES 3 DOZEN COOKIES ❋ Bite into these buttery, nutty cookies, and you're greeted with a little surprise: a Frango Chocolate center. The cake flour makes them extra light and tender.

**1 cup (2 sticks) unsalted butter, at room temperature**

**1/2 cup confectioners' sugar, plus more for rolling**

**2 cups cake flour**

**1 teaspoon vanilla extract**

**Pinch of salt**

**1 cup finely chopped pecans**

**18 Frango Chocolates (Mint, Dark Mint, Double Chocolate, or Dark Chocolate), halved crosswise**

In a bowl, using an electric mixer, cream together the butter and confectioners' sugar on medium-high speed for about 1 minute, or until the mixture is pale yellow and fluffy. Add the flour, vanilla, and salt and stir with a wooden spoon until well blended. Stir in the pecans. Cover the bowl with plastic wrap and refrigerate for about 1 hour, or until the dough is firm.

Position racks in the center and top of the oven and preheat to 350°F. Scoop out a level tablespoon of dough and shape it around a chocolate half, enclosing the chocolate completely. Roll the dough between your palms to form a ball. Repeat with the remaining dough and chocolates. As the cookies are shaped, arrange them on ungreased baking sheets, spacing them about 1 inch apart.

Bake for 18 to 20 minutes, switching the pans between the racks and rotating them 180 degrees about halfway through baking, or until the cookies are golden brown. Meanwhile, sift confectioners' sugar into a small bowl. When the cookies are ready, remove from the oven, let them cool just until they can be handled, and then roll them in the sugar, coating them well. Put them on a rack and let cool completely. The cookies can be stored in an airtight container at room temperature for up to 1 week.

# Merangos

MAKES ABOUT 16 COOKIES ❋ These sophisticated, fudgy confections are the cookie cousin of flourless chocolate cake. With just five staples (assuming you're someone who considers Frango Dark Chocolates a staple), they're easy to whip up on a moment's notice—just the thing for when friends drop in unexpectedly or a sudden chocolate-cookie craving strikes. They're made like meringues, but, thanks to the Frangos, they're much denser and richer.

**18 Frango Dark Chocolates, melted (page 8)**

**2 egg whites**

**$1/_4$ teaspoon salt**

**$1/_2$ cup sugar**

**1 teaspoon vanilla extract**

Position racks in the center and top of the oven and preheat to 350°F. Line 2 baking sheets with parchment paper.

Allow the chocolate to cool for a few minutes, or until tepid. Meanwhile, using an electric mixer, beat the egg whites on low speed until foamy. Add the salt and increase the speed to medium. Beat for about 1 minute, or until the egg whites are fluffy and hold soft peaks. Increase the speed to high and add the sugar, a few tablespoons at a time, beating for 3 to 5 minutes, or until the egg whites are glossy and hold stiff peaks.

Using a rubber spatula, gently fold the chocolate and vanilla into the egg whites just until combined. Spoon by rounded tablespoons onto the prepared pans, spacing them 2 inches apart.

Bake for 12 to 14 minutes, switching the pans between the racks and rotating them 180 degrees about halfway through baking, or until the cookies are dry and crisp on top and moist in the center when tested with a toothpick. Do not overbake. Let cool completely on the pans on racks. The cookies can be stored in an airtight container at room temperature for up to 2 days.

# Frango Brownie Bites

MAKES 2 DOZEN SMALL BROWNIES ✳ Sometimes all the brownie you want is just a single perfect bite. These little gems deliver—with the triple satisfaction of chocolate, coffee, and caramel. You can also bake this batter in a greased 8-inch square pan for 22 to 25 minutes, or until a toothpick inserted in the center comes out clean.

- **$1/2$ cup (1 stick) unsalted butter**
- **15 Frango Dark Chocolates**
- **1 cup sugar**
- **2 eggs, lightly beaten**
- **1 teaspoon vanilla extract**
- **1 teaspoon instant espresso powder**
- **$1/2$ cup all-purpose flour**
- **1 tablespoon cocoa powder**
- **9 Frango Chocolates (Double Chocolate or Caramel), quartered**
- **$1/8$ teaspoon salt**
- **Vanilla or caramel ice cream, for serving (optional)**

Position a rack in the center of the oven and preheat to 350°F. Grease a 24-portion mini-muffin pan with nonstick spray.

In a heavy-bottomed saucepan, melt the butter over medium heat. Remove from the heat and add the Dark Chocolates, stirring until they are melted and smooth. Add the sugar, eggs, vanilla, and espresso powder and stir until the mixture is well combined and smooth. Sift in the flour and cocoa powder and stir just until combined. Stir in the Double Chocolates or Caramel Chocolates. Divide the batter evenly among the prepared muffin cups, filling them about three-fourths full.

Bake for about 12 minutes, or until a toothpick inserted in the center of a brownie comes out clean. Let cool to room temperature on a rack before unmolding. Serve with ice cream, or store in an airtight container at room temperature for up to 4 days.

# Easy Frango Refrigerator Cookies

EACH RECIPE MAKES 40 COOKIES ❄ All it takes is a few Frango Chocolates to turn store-bought refrigerated cookie dough into something special.

## FRANGO SUGAR COOKIES

**1 (18-ounce) package Pillsbury or other refrigerated pull-apart cookie dough**

**20 Frango Chocolates (Mint, Double Chocolate, Dark Chocolate, or Caramel), halved crosswise**

Position racks in the center and top of the oven and preheat to 325°F.

Separate the dough into squares, and cut each square in half. Arrange the dough pieces on 2 ungreased baking sheets, spacing them 2 inches apart. Press a chocolate half, cut side up, in the center of each dough piece.

Bake for about 12 minutes, switching the pans between the racks and rotating them 180 degrees about halfway through baking, or until the cookies are just starting to brown. Let cool completely on the pans on racks. Do not stack the cookies until the chocolate has cooled completely and hardened. The cookies can be stored in an airtight container at room temperature for up to 4 days.

**1 (16.5-ounce) roll Pillsbury or other refrigerated peanut butter cookie dough**

**Sugar, for rolling**

**20 Frango Double Chocolates, halved crosswise**

Position racks in the center and top of the oven and preheat to 350°F.

Cut the dough crosswise into 4 equal pieces, and then cut each piece into 10 equal slices. Place the sugar in a small bowl. Roll each dough slice between your palms to make a 1-inch ball, then roll the ball in the sugar, coating evenly. As the balls are coated, arrange them on 2 ungreased baking sheets, spacing them 2 inches apart. Flatten the balls with a fork, creating a crosshatch pattern. Press a chocolate half, cut side up, into the center of each cookie.

Bake for about 12 minutes, switching the pans between the racks and rotating them 180 degrees about halfway through baking, or until the cookies are just beginning to brown. Let cool completely on the pans on racks. Do not stack the cookies until the chocolate has cooled completely and hardened. The cookies can be stored in an airtight container at room temperature for up to 4 days.

# Mint Chocolate Chip Cookies

MAKES ABOUT 8 DOZEN COOKIES ✳ Ready to take a break from "this old Toll House"? Instead of the usual chips and walnuts, these chewy cookies are studded with chunks of Frango Mint Chocolates and pecans.

**2¹/₄ cups all-purpose flour**

**1 teaspoon baking soda**

**¹/₂ teaspoon salt**

**¹/₂ cup (1 stick) unsalted butter, at room temperature**

**¹/₂ cup solid vegetable shortening, at room temperature**

**1 cup firmly packed light brown sugar**

**¹/₂ cup granulated sugar**

**2 eggs, at room temperature**

**5 Frango Mint Chocolates, very finely chopped**

**1 teaspoon vanilla extract**

**25 Frango Mint Chocolates, coarsely chopped**

**³/₄ cup coarsely chopped pecans**

Position racks in the center and top of the oven and preheat to 350°F. Line 2 baking sheets with parchment paper, or use nonstick sheets.

Sift together the flour, baking soda, and salt into a bowl. Put the butter and shortening in a separate large bowl. Using an electric mixer, cream the butter and shortening on medium speed for about 1 minute, or until well blended. Add both sugars and beat for about 1 minute, or until well mixed. Beat in the eggs, finely chopped chocolates, and vanilla. Add the flour mixture and stir with a wooden spoon until well blended. Stir in the coarsely chopped chocolates and pecans. Drop the dough by rounded teaspoons onto the prepared pans, spacing them 1 inch apart.

Bake for about 10 minutes, or until the cookies are firm at the edges and soft in the center. Transfer the cookies to racks and let cool completely. Repeat with the remaining dough. The cookies can be stored in an airtight container at room temperature for up to 5 days.

# Frango-Dipped Treats

Frango Chocolates contain everything you need to create professional-looking chocolate-coated treats. If you like making homemade gifts, these are as easy as "melt and dip."

## CHOCOLATE PRETZELS

MAKES 24 PRETZELS ✴ Sweet-salty never tasted better. Use this same technique for dipping candy canes. (Pictured on page 22.)

**30 Frango Chocolates (Mint, Dark Mint, Double Chocolate, or Dark Chocolate), melted (page 8)**

**24 pretzel rods**

**Chocolate sprinkles, finely chopped Frango Chocolates, and/or finely chopped toasted nuts (page 10), for garnish**

Put the chocolate in a tall, narrow drinking glass. Dip a pretzel about three-fourths of the way into the chocolate, allowing the excess chocolate to drip back into the glass. Place on a waxed paper–lined baking sheet. Repeat with the remaining pretzels. As the chocolate is depleted, you may need to tilt the glass to coat the last few pretzels.

While the chocolate is still warm, sprinkle the chosen garnish(es) on the pretzels. Let set for about 4 hours, or until the chocolate has hardened. The pretzels will keep in an airtight container at room temperature for a week or more.

## FRANGO MANGOES

MAKES 24 CANDIES ✴ These easy-to-make candies are elegant enough to give as a gift or to serve with coffee and after-dinner drinks at a special meal. You can also use other dried fruits, such as apricots or pears, or cookies, such as biscotti or amaretti.

**15 Frango Chocolates (Double Chocolate or Dark Chocolate), melted (page 8)**

**24 pieces dried mango (about 7 ounces)**

**¹/₄ cup finely chopped salted roasted pistachios, for garnish**

Put the chocolate in a coffee cup. Dip a mango piece about halfway into the chocolate, allowing the excess chocolate to drip back into the cup. Place on a waxed paper–lined baking sheet. Repeat with the remaining mango pieces. As the chocolate is depleted, you may need to tilt the cup to coat the last few mango pieces.

While the chocolate is still warm, sprinkle with the pistachios. Let set for about 4 hours, or until the chocolate has hardened. The mango pieces will keep in an airtight container at room temperature for up to 1 week.

## WHITE CHOCOLATE DRIZZLE

MAKES ENOUGH TO GARNISH ABOUT 24 TREATS ✴ Use this simple method to give Frango-dipped confections a professional-looking finish.

**1 (3.5-ounce) bar white chocolate, melted (page 8)**

Using a rapid back-and-forth motion, drizzle the chocolate from the tip of a spoon over the confection you want to decorate. (You can practice over waxed paper until you achieve attractive, uniform lines of chocolate, then scoop up the chocolate and return it to the bowl or pan.) Let set at room temperature for about 4 hours, or until the chocolate has hardened. You can drizzle on the white chocolate while the chocolate used for dipping is still warm and soft.

## CHOCOLATE MELTAWAY SPOONS

MAKES 24 CHOCOLATE SPOONS ✳ Designed to add flavor as you use them to stir hot coffee or chocolate, these spoons make a fun gift. Look for bamboo or wooden spoons at natural-foods stores.

**30 Frango Chocolates (Mint, Double Chocolate,
   or Dark Chocolate), melted  (page 8)**

**24 disposable spoons**

**Finely chopped Frango Chocolates, miniature
   marshmallows, and/or whole Frango Chocolates,
   for garnish**

Put the chocolate in a tall, narrow drinking glass. Dip a spoon about halfway into the chocolate, allowing the excess chocolate to drip back into the glass. Place on a waxed paper–lined baking sheet. Repeat with the remaining spoons. As the chocolate is depleted, you may need to tilt the glass to coat the last few spoons.

While the chocolate is still warm, finish the spoons in one of three ways: sprinkle chopped Frango Chocolates over the melted chocolate; place 3 marshmallows in the bowl of each spoon and sprinkle with chopped Frango Chocolates; or place 1 whole Frango Chocolate in the bowl of each spoon. Let set for about 4 hours, or until the chocolate has hardened. The spoons will keep in an airtight container at room temperature for a week or more.

# Frango Cone-acopia

MAKES 6 CONES ✳ Serve these Frango-dipped cones filled with ice cream, or turn them into gifts by stuffing them with Frango Chocolates, wrapping them in clear floral cellophane cones (the kind used for bouquets, available at floral-supply stores), and tying the tops with a pretty ribbon. Buy the waffle cones from an ice cream shop.

**6 large waffle cones**

**20 Frango Chocolates (Mint, Dark Mint, Double Chocolate, or Dark Chocolate), melted (page 8)**

**$^1/_2$ cup toasted sliced almonds (page 10), $^1/_4$ cup sprinkles, and/or $^1/_2$ cup finely chopped Frango Chocolates, for garnish**

Dip the open end of a cone about 1 inch deep into the chocolate, allowing the excess chocolate to drip back into the bowl. Stand the cone right side up in a tall glass and let cool for 2 to 3 minutes, then remove from the glass and sprinkle the chosen garnish(es) onto the chocolate. Return the cone to the glass and repeat with the remaining cones.

Pour the remaining chocolate into the bottoms of the cones, dividing it evenly. Let set at room temperature for about 4 hours, or until the chocolate has hardened. The cones will keep in an airtight container at room temperature for up to 1 week.

# Frango Ganache

MAKES 1 CUP ✳ Melt Frango Chocolates in heavy cream and you've got a rich mixture known as ganache, which you can use for making homemade truffles, filling sandwich cookies, or pouring warm over cakes, cupcakes, or cheesecakes for a satiny glaze. Heat the cream and chocolate with care, just until the chocolate melts. When reheating ganache (in a double boiler or in the microwave) to use as a glaze, heat gradually and avoid overheating, which can cause it to become grainy.

**¹/₂ cup heavy cream**

**24 Frango Chocolates (Mint, Dark Mint, Double Chocolate, or Dark Chocolate), chopped**

In a small saucepan, heat the cream over medium heat just until it comes to a boil. Stir in the chocolates, remove from the heat, and stir until they melt and the mixture is smooth. Use warm as a glaze, or let cool, cover, and refrigerate for up to 1 week.

## FRANGANACHE TRUFFLES

MAKES 2 DOZEN TRUFFLES ✳ These truffles need to be stored in the refrigerator, but they taste best at room temperature, when they're meltingly soft and their flavor is at its most intense.

**2 tablespoons cocoa powder**

**2 tablespoons finely chopped toasted walnuts or almonds (page 10)**

**1 cup Frango Ganache (above), at room temperature**

Put the cocoa powder and nuts in separate small bowls. Using a melon baller or a teaspoon, scoop up a heaping teaspoon of ganache and roll it between your palms to make a ball. Repeat with the remaining ganache to make 2 dozen truffles in all. Roll 12 of the truffles in the cocoa powder and the other 12 truffles in the nuts, coating them evenly. Put the truffles on a plate, cover loosely with plastic wrap, and refrigerate for 1 to 2 hours, or until firm. Transfer the truffles to an airtight container and refrigerate for up to 1 week.

# Frango Rice Krispie Treats

MAKES 12 LARGE BARS ❊ For years, these Rice Krispie bars, topped with a layer of Frango Chocolates, have been written up in newspapers, featured on TV, discussed on the Internet, and enjoyed by thousands of shoppers at Marshall Field's, and now Macy's. Here's the easy, no-bake recipe.

**6 tablespoons unsalted butter**

**1 (16-ounce) package miniature marshmallows**

**8 cups crispy rice cereal**

**36 Frango Chocolates (Mint, Dark Mint, Double Chocolate, or Dark Chocolate), chopped**

Butter a 9-by-13-inch baking pan. In a large, heavy-bottomed saucepan, melt the butter over medium heat. Add the marshmallows and stir constantly for about 5 minutes, or until completely melted and smooth. Watch carefully to avoid burning, and reduce the heat if the mixture begins to brown.

Remove from the heat, add the cereal, and stir well to combine thoroughly. Scoop the mixture into the prepared pan. Butter your hands and firmly pat the mixture into the pan, making as even a layer as possible. Sprinkle the chocolates over the top and spread them in an even layer with a rubber spatula. (The heat from the cereal mixture should soften the chocolate enough to spread it; if not, place the pan in a warm oven for 2 minutes to soften the chocolate.)

Let set for 4 to 6 hours, or until the chocolate has hardened, before cutting into 12 bars. The bars can be stored in an airtight container at room temperature for up to 3 days.

# Oven S'mores

MAKES 9 S'MORES ✳ No campfire? No problem. Macy's Culinary Council chef Gale Gand came up with this easy way to experience s'more satisfaction anytime. These treats are ideal for making with kids because there's no measuring or mixing (though an adult should do the final sandwiching step). Of course, they're best warm, but they're also good at room temperature.

**9 whole graham crackers**

**9 marshmallows**

**9 Frango Chocolates (Double Chocolate or Dark Chocolate)**

Position a rack in the center of the oven and preheat to 400°F. Break each graham cracker in half and arrange the 18 pieces on a baking sheet. Place a marshmallow in the center of 9 of the crackers, and a chocolate in the center of the remaining 9 crackers.

Bake for 4 minutes, or until the marshmallows are puffed and golden and the chocolates are soft. Remove from the oven. Sandwich together the chocolate sides with the marshmallow sides, pressing gently to spread the filling. Serve immediately, or let cool completely and store in an airtight container at room temperature for up to 1 day.

# Frango Hot Chocolate

SERVES 4 ✳ If you can boil water (or in this case milk), you can make this rich, creamy hot cocoa. It's nothing more than Frango Chocolates and hot milk whipped in a blender, but you'll be amazed by its velvety richness.

**9 Frango Chocolates (Mint, Dark Mint, Double Chocolate, or Dark Chocolate), chopped, plus more for garnish**

**3 cups milk, heated just to a boil**

Put the chocolates in a blender and pour in the hot milk. Place the lid on the blender and cover it with a folded dish towel. Holding the lid firmly in place to keep the hot liquid from spattering, process on high speed for 15 seconds, or until the chocolates and milk are well blended and the mixture is frothy.

Divide among 4 warmed mugs. Using a vegetable peeler, garnish each serving with chocolate shavings. Serve immediately.

# Cakes & Pies

# Quick Frango Frosting

MAKES ENOUGH TO FROST 24 CUPCAKES, ONE 8-INCH ROUND TWO-
LAYER CAKE, OR ONE 9-BY-13-INCH CAKE ✳ Who says fluffy
buttercream-style frosting has to be tricky to make? This version is
fast, foolproof, and Frango fabulous.

> **24 Frango Chocolates (Mint, Dark Mint, Double
>  Chocolate, or Dark Chocolate), melted (page 8)**
>
> **4 cups confectioners' sugar**
>
> **$1/2$ cup (1 stick) butter, at room temperature**
>
> **$3/4$ cup milk**

Allow the chocolate to cool for a few minutes, or until tepid. Using
an electric mixer fitted with the paddle attachment, beat together
the chocolate, sugar, butter, and milk on low speed until combined.
Increase the speed to high and beat for 3 to 5 minutes, or until the
mixture is light, fluffy, and smooth. Use immediately.

# Flourless Frango Chocolate Cakes

SERVES 6 ✳ Do you love those warm, ultrarich chocolate cakes so many restaurants are serving nowadays? This home version, created by Macy's Corporate chef Tim Scott, is made with just three ingredients. Instead of ramekins, you can make it in an 8-inch round cake pan (bake as directed, let cool, and invert onto a plate to unmold). Either way, watch carefully and err on the side of underbaking, so the center is a bit runny. Serve warm with whippped cream or vanilla ice cream.

**45 (1-pound box) Frango Chocolates (Mint, Dark Mint, Double Chocolate, or Dark Chocolate)**

**1 cup (2 sticks) unsalted butter**

**6 eggs**

Position a rack in the center of the oven and preheat to 425°F. Generously grease six 1-cup ramekins or heatproof custard cups with nonstick spray or butter.

Pour water to a depth of about 2 inches into a saucepan and bring to a bare simmer. Combine the chocolates and butter in a heatproof bowl that fits snugly in the rim of the pan, and place over, but not touching, the simmering water. Heat, stirring often, for 5 to 7 minutes, or until melted and smooth. Remove the bowl from the heat.

Break the eggs into a separate heatproof bowl and whisk just until blended. Place over, but not touching, the barely simmering water. Heat, stirring constantly, just until warm to the touch. Remove the bowl from the heat. Using an electric mixer, beat the eggs on high speed until light and foamy. Fold the eggs into the chocolate mixture just until completely combined. Divide the mixture evenly among the prepared ramekins. Set the ramekins on a baking sheet.

Bake for 5 minutes, then cover with aluminum foil and bake for 15 minutes longer. Remove from the oven and serve immediately, or let cool to room temperature before serving.

# Angel Food Whipped Cream Cake

SERVES 8 TO 10 ✳ Need a showstopping dessert in a pinch? This one, made with two shortcut ingredients (store-bought angel food cake and Frango Mint Chocolate Dessert Topping), can be whipped up in just a few minutes.

> **1 store-bought angel food cake**
>
> **2 cups heavy cream**
>
> **1 (15-ounce) jar Frango Mint Chocolate Dessert Topping**
>
> **12 Frango Chocolates (Mint, Dark Mint, Dark Chocolate, or Double Chocolate), chopped**

Using a serrated knife, carefully slice the cake horizontally into 3 equal layers.

Using an electric mixer, whip the cream on medium-high speed until it barely holds soft peaks. Pour in the dessert topping and mix on low speed until thoroughly combined, then continue mixing for 30 to 45 seconds, or until the cream holds stiff peaks. Stir the mixture with a rubber scraper to evenly distribute any sauce that may have sunk to the bottom of the bowl.

Place the bottom cake layer on a serving platter. Spread one-fourth of the cream mixture over the top. Sprinkle with one-fourth of the chopped chocolates, and top with the second layer. Spread one-third of the remaining cream mixture over the second layer, and sprinkle with one-third of the remaining chocolates. Top with the third cake layer. Frost the top and sides of the cake with the remaining cream mixture, then sprinkle the top and sides with the remaining chocolates. Serve immediately, or cover loosely, refrigerate for up to 8 hours, and serve chilled.

# Turtle Pie

SERVES 8 ✳ If you're partial to pecan pie, try this Frango-enhanced version, which combines four of the all-time greatest dessert flavors: chocolate, nuts, caramel, and whipped cream.

**³/₄ cup (1¹/₂ sticks) butter**

**³/₄ cup firmly packed light brown sugar**

**6 tablespoons light corn syrup**

**¹/₄ cup heavy cream**

**3 cups pecan  halves, slivered almonds, or chopped walnuts, toasted (page 10)**

**6 Frango Dark Chocolates**

**1 (9-inch) store-bought chocolate crumb pie crust**

**Whipped cream, for garnish**

**4 Frango Caramel Chocolates, halved crosswise, for garnish**

Position a rack in the center of the oven and preheat to 350°F.

In a heavy-bottomed saucepan, combine the butter, sugar, and corn syrup over medium heat. Bring to a boil and boil for 1 minute, stirring constantly. Stir in the cream and nuts and continue to boil and stir for 3 minutes. Remove from the heat, add the Dark Chocolates, and stir until they are melted and fully incorporated. Pour into the pie crust.

Bake for 8 for 10 minutes, or until the filling is bubbling. Let cool on a rack to room temperature. The pie can be covered and refrigerated for up to 2 days; bring to room temperature before serving. To serve, cut into 8 slices and garnish each slice with a dollop of whipped cream and a Caramel Chocolate half.

# Hazelnut Chocolate Coffee Cake

SERVES 8 TO 10 ✳ A classic American sour cream coffee cake—moist and rich, with a nutty chocolate layer hidden in the center. Perfect for a weekend family brunch or for bringing to a potluck.

> **1 cup (2 sticks) unsalted butter, melted and slightly cooled**
>
> **2 cups granulated sugar**
>
> **2 eggs, lightly beaten**
>
> **1 cup sour cream**
>
> **1 teaspoon vanilla extract**
>
> **1$^1$/$_2$ cups all-purpose flour**
>
> **$^1$/$_4$ cup wheat germ**
>
> **1 teaspoon salt**
>
> **1 teaspoon baking powder**
>
> **$^1$/$_2$ cup toasted, skinned, and chopped hazelnuts (page 10)**
>
> **1 tablespoon firmly packed dark brown sugar**
>
> **1 teaspoon ground cinnamon**
>
> **8 Frango Chocolates (Double Chocolate or Dark Chocolate), coarsely chopped**

Position a rack in the center of the oven and preheat to 350°F. Grease a 10-cup nonstick Bundt pan with nonstick spray.

In a large bowl, combine the butter, granulated sugar, eggs, sour cream, and vanilla and mix well with a wooden spoon. Stir in the flour, wheat germ, salt, and baking powder just until combined. Do not over-mix. In a small bowl, combine the hazelnuts, brown sugar, and cinnamon and toss to mix well.

Sprinkle half of the nut mixture in the bottom of the prepared pan. Pour half of the batter over the nut mixture. Sprinkle on the remaining nut mixture, followed by the chopped chocolates. Pour in the remaining batter. Bake for 50 to 60 minutes, or until the cake is firm to the touch and golden brown on top. Let cool in the pan on a rack for 10 minutes, then invert onto a serving platter to unmold. Serve warm or at room temperature.

# Famous Frango Chocolate Cheesecake

SERVES 8 ✳ This is a much-loved specialty from the Walnut Room: a mint chocolate cheesecake with a Frango–sour cream topping and a semisweet chocolate glaze. Be sure to allow plenty of time for the baking, cooling, topping, and glazing steps.

## CRUST

1 cup chocolate wafer cookie crumbs such as Nabisco Famous Chocolate Wafers (about 20 cookies)

4 tablespoons unsalted butter, melted

1 tablespoon plus 2 teaspoons sugar

## FILLING

15 Frango Mint Chocolates, melted (page 8)

3 (8-ounce) packages cream cheese, at room temperature

1 cup sugar

2 eggs, at room temperature

$1/3$ cup heavy cream

$1/2$ teaspoon vanilla extract

## TOPPING

$1/4$ teaspoon unflavored gelatin

1 tablespoon cold water

3 Frango Mint Chocolates, finely chopped

$1/2$ cup sour cream, at room temperature

## GLAZE

$3/4$ cup heavy cream

3 ounces semisweet chocolate, finely chopped

2 tablespoons unsalted butter

Whipped cream, for serving

8 mint sprigs, for garnish

continued

Position a rack in the center of the oven and preheat to 350°F.

**Crust:** In a food processor, combine the cookie crumbs, butter, and sugar. Process until well blended. Transfer to an ungreased 8-inch springform pan with 2-inch sides and press firmly into the bottom.

**Filling:** Allow the chocolate to cool for a few minutes, or until tepid. Place the cream cheese in a large bowl. Using an electric mixer, beat on medium speed until smooth. Add the sugar and beat until blended. Add the eggs one at a time, blending well after each addition and stopping as needed to scrape down the bowl sides and the beaters. Add the chocolate, cream, and vanilla and beat until well mixed. Pour the batter into the crust.

Bake for about 35 minutes, or until the sides of the cake rise and the top jiggles slightly when the pan is shaken. (The cake will appear underbaked, but will firm on chilling.) Remove from the oven, run a sharp knife around the inside of the pan to loosen the cake from the pan sides, and let cool completely in the pan on a rack.

**Topping:** Pour water to a depth of about 2 inches into a saucepan and heat until it is steaming but not simmering. Meanwhile, combine the gelatin and cold water in a heatproof bowl that fits snugly in the rim of the pan and let stand for about 5 minutes, or until the gelatin has softened. Place the bowl over, but not touching, the steaming water and stir for about 3 minutes, or until the gelatin has dissolved. Add the chocolates and stir for 2 to 3 minutes, or until melted. Remove from the heat and allow to cool until tepid. Whisk the sour cream into the chocolate mixture until blended. Spread the topping evenly on top of the cheesecake. Refrigerate for 4 hours, or until well chilled.

**Glaze:** In a small saucepan, bring the cream to a boil over medium-high heat. Remove from the heat, add the chocolate, and stir until melted. Add the butter and whisk until melted. Let the glaze stand at room temperature for about 30 minutes, or until cooled and thickened. With the sides of the springform pan still in place, pour the glaze evenly over the cheesecake, then refrigerate for about 30 minutes, or until set. (Or, cover and refrigerate for up to 2 days.)

To serve, remove the pan sides, slice the cake, and top each serving with a dollop of whipped cream and a mint sprig.

# Special Occasions

# Frango Fountain

SERVES 8 TO 12 ✳ No matter what else you serve at a festive dinner, buffet, or brunch, if the dessert is chocolate fondue or its splashier cousin, a chocolate fountain, that's what everyone will remember. Dipping sweet morsels into melted chocolate is fun, interactive, and decadent. And Frango Chocolate Melts—chocolate disks created especially for melting and dipping, with no need for other ingredients—make a fountain or fondue easy.

Electric chocolate fountains for home use are available in the housewares department of Macy's and other major department stores. You pour in melted chocolate, and the mechanism in the base keeps the chocolate warm and sends it cascading over the top in a shimmering, tiered curtain. Consult the manufacturers' directions to determine how much chocolate your fountain can hold. Plan on a total of about 1 cup of the various dipping ingredients per person.

**2 (24-ounce) packages Frango Chocolate Melts (Double Chocolate or Dark Chocolate), or more depending on the size of the fountain**

DIPPING INGREDIENTS FOR ADULTS

**Angel food or pound cake, cut into 1-inch cubes**

**Small cookies such as shortbread or macaroons**

**Biscotti**

**Strawberries**

**Seedless grapes**

**Banana slices**

**Pineapple chunks**

**Orange segments**

**Cherries, pitted**

**Dried apricots**

continued

**Animal crackers**

**Graham crackers**

**Apple wedges**

**Seedless grapes**

**Licorice twists**

**Marshmallows**

**Gummi Bears or Swedish Fish**

Set up a chocolate fountain or fondue dish on a buffet station or dining table, making sure the surface is stable, then secure the fountain's electrical cord with tape. Melt the chocolate disks according to the package directions, and fill the fountain or dish. Arrange a variety of dipping ingredients around the base, along with fondue forks or disposable wooden skewers and plenty of cocktail napkins.

# Frango One-Two Mousse

SERVES 6  ❋  It takes just two ingredients—Frango Chocolates and heavy cream—to make fluffy, restaurant-style chocolate mousse. This mousse tastes best at room temperature, but it's so easy, you can make it just before serving. Or prepare it ahead of time and let it come to room temperature as directed.

**28 Frango Double Chocolates**

**2 cups heavy cream**

**Berries, for garnish**

**Whipped cream, for garnish**

**Small cookies, for garnish**

Melt the chocolates in a large, heatproof bowl as directed on page 8. Allow to cool for a few minutes, or until tepid. Meanwhile, using an electric mixer, whip the cream on high speed just until it holds stiff peaks.

Whisk one-third of the whipped cream into the chocolate to lighten it. Using a rubber spatula, gently fold in the remaining whipped cream in two additions just until combined. Do not overmix.

Spoon the mixture into a pastry bag fitted with a large plain or star tip, or into a 1-gallon resealable plastic bag and snip off a bottom corner. Pipe the mousse into 6 dessert glasses or bowls. Serve immediately, or cover and refrigerate for up to 4 days, then bring to room temperature (about 1 hour) before serving. Garnish with the berries, whipped cream, and cookies.

# Tiramisù Torta

SERVES 8 TO 12 ❊ Tiramisù rises to new heights of elegance when you make it in a springform pan. If you'd rather use a baking dish, see the variation on the next page. Either crisp ladyfingers, such as Italian *savoiardi* (Savoy biscuits), or refrigerated soft ladyfingers can be used.

> 1½ cups heavy cream
>
> 1 (15-ounce) jar Frango Double Chocolate Dessert Topping
>
> 1 (16-ounce) container mascarpone cheese, at room temperature
>
> 1½ cups warm water
>
> 2 tablespoons instant espresso powder
>
> ½ cup coffee liqueur such as Kahlúa
>
> 12 to 14 ounces crisp or soft ladyfingers
>
> 8 Frango Dark Chocolates, finely chopped
>
> Frango Chocolate shavings and cocoa powder, for garnish

Using an electric mixer, whip the cream on medium-high speed until it almost holds soft peaks. Turn off the mixer and pour in the dessert topping. Whip on medium-high speed again until the topping is fully incorporated and the cream holds stiff peaks. Do not overwhip.

Put the mascarpone in a large bowl and stir with a whisk to soften. Thoroughly fold in one-third of the cream mixture to lighten the mascarpone. Then fold in the remaining cream mixture in two additions just until combined.

In a small bowl, stir together the water and espresso powder until the powder has dissolved, then stir in the liqueur. One at a time, dip the ladyfingers into the espresso mixture for 5 to 7 seconds if using crisp ladyfingers, and less time if using soft ones. They should be well moistened, but their centers should still be firm. As you dip the cookies, begin arranging them in the bottom of a 9-inch springform pan with 2½- to 4-inch sides, covering it completely. Stand more dipped ladyfingers on end, side by side, to line the sides of the pan.

continued

Spread half of the mascarpone mixture in the lined pan. Sprinkle with half of the chopped chocolates, and then cover with another layer of dipped ladyfingers. Top with the remaining mascarpone mixture and sprinkle on the remaining chopped chocolate. Garnish with Frango Chocolate shavings made with a vegetable peeler, and dust with cocoa powder. Cover with plastic wrap and refrigerate for about 2 hours, or until firm.

Remove the pan sides and, if desired, tie a decorative ribbon around the torta. To serve, remove the ribbon and slice the torta into wedges. The torta will keep in the refrigerator for up to 3 days.

**Variation:** This recipe can be prepared in a 9-by-13-inch baking dish. You'll need 16 chopped Frangos, because there's more surface area to cover. Line the bottom of the dish with a layer of dipped ladyfingers, spread half of the mascarpone mixture on top, and sprinkle on half of the chopped chocolates. Repeat the layers, using the remaining ladyfingers, mascarpone mixture, and chocolates. Cover and refrigerate as directed. Cut into 8 to 12 servings.

# Frango Chocolate Pudding

SERVES 6  ✳ This homemade pudding makes a nice everyday treat. Layer it in tall glasses with a few easy-to-find ingredients, and it becomes a company-worthy dessert. Each of the parfait recipes makes 8 desserts. Use 12- to 14-ounce parfait or pilsner glasses.

  **¹/₂ cup sugar**

  **¹/₄ cup cocoa powder**

  **3 tablespoons cornstarch**

  **¹/₄ teaspoon salt**

  **3 cups milk**

  **15 Frango Double Chocolates, chopped**

  **1 teaspoon vanilla extract**

In a heavy-bottomed saucepan, whisk together the sugar, cocoa powder, cornstarch, and salt until well combined. Whisk in 1 cup of the milk until smooth. Whisk in the remaining 2 cups milk and place over medium heat. Bring to a boil, whisking constantly. Boil for 1 minute, then remove from the heat. Add the chocolates and vanilla and whisk until the chocolates are melted and the mixture is smooth.

Divide the pudding among 6 dessert bowls. Refrigerate for 30 minutes before serving, or cover with plastic wrap (press the wrap directly on top of the pudding to keep it from forming a skin) and refrigerate for up to 2 days.

## CHOCOLATE BANANA CREAM PARFAITS
(Pictured on page 56)

Using an electric mixer, whip 2 cups heavy cream with 2 tablespoons sugar on high speed until stiff peaks form. Stir in 1 tablespoon dark rum. Spoon 1 recipe chilled Frango Chocolate Pudding (above) into a pastry bag fitted with a large plain tip, or into a 1-gallon resealable plastic bag and snip off one bottom corner. Pipe about ¹/₄ cup pudding into the bottom of each of 8 glasses. Slice 4 bananas and divide half of the slices among the glasses, followed by half of the whipped

continued

cream. Repeat with the remaining pudding, banana slices, and whipped cream. Top each parfait with toasted coconut and Frango Chocolate shavings made with a vegetable peeler. Serve immediately, or cover, refrigerate for up to 1 hour, and serve chilled.

## CHOCOLATE STRAWBERRY PARFAITS

Using an electric mixer, whip 2 cups heavy cream with 2 tablespoons sugar on high speed until stiff peaks form. Spoon 1 recipe chilled Frango Chocolate Pudding (page 55) into a pastry bag fitted with a large plain tip, or into a 1-gallon resealable plastic bag and snip off one bottom corner. Pipe about $1/4$ cup pudding into the bottom of each of 8 glasses. Cut store-bought angel food cake into $3/4$-inch cubes to total 2 cups. Divide half of the cubes among the glasses. Slice strawberries to total 2 cups. Layer half of the slices in the glasses, followed by half of the whipped cream. Repeat with the remaining pudding, cake cubes, strawberry slices, and whipped cream. Chop 4 Frango Chocolates (the same flavor used for the pudding) and sprinkle evenly over the parfaits. Serve immediately, or cover, refrigerate for up to 1 hour, and serve chilled.

## BLACK & WHITE COOKIE PARFAITS

Using an electric mixer, whip 2 cups heavy cream with 2 tablespoons sugar on high speed until stiff peaks form. Spoon 1 recipe chilled Frango Chocolate Pudding (page 55) into a pastry bag fitted with a large plain tip, or into a 1-gallon resealable plastic bag and snip off one bottom corner. Pipe about $1/4$ cup pudding into the bottom of each of 8 glasses. Coarsely chop 32 chocolate sandwich cookies (such as Oreos). Divide half of the cookies among the glasses. Layer half of the whipped cream over the cookies. Repeat with the remaining pudding and cookies, reserving a few tablespoons of cookies for garnish. Divide the remaining whipped cream among the glasses, and sprinkle the reserved cookies on top. Serve immediately, or cover, refrigerate for up to 1 hour, and serve chilled.

# Warm Frango Soufflé

SERVES 6 TO 8 ✳ A classic dark chocolate soufflé that comes to the table dramatically puffed, piping hot, and with a soft, creamy center.

**1 tablespoon butter, for coating the soufflé dish**

**¹/₂ cup granulated sugar, plus more for coating the soufflé dish**

**4 egg yolks**

**20 Frango Dark Chocolates, melted (page 8)**

**2 tablespoons Frangelico, Grand Marnier, or amaretto**

**1 teaspoon vanilla extract**

**8 egg whites**

**¹/₄ teaspoon cream of tartar**

**Pinch of salt**

**Confectioners' sugar, for dusting**

**Vanilla ice cream, for serving**

**Frango Fudge Sauce (page 69), warmed, for serving (optional)**

Position a rack in the center of the oven and preheat to 375°F. Grease the bottom and sides of a 2-quart soufflé dish with the butter. Sprinkle with granulated sugar, rotate the dish to coat it evenly, and then invert, tapping out the excess.

One at a time, whisk the egg yolks into the melted chocolate, mixing thoroughly after each addition. Stir in the liqueur and vanilla.

In a large bowl, using an electric mixer, beat together the egg whites, cream of tartar, and salt on medium speed for about 1 minute, or just until the whites hold soft peaks. Add the granulated sugar, a few tablespoons at a time, continuing to beat on medium speed. When all the sugar has been added, increase the speed to high and beat for about 2 minutes more, or until the whites hold stiff peaks. Whisk one-fourth of the whites into the chocolate mixture to lighten it, then gently fold the chocolate mixture into the remaining whites just until combined. Gently transfer the mixture to the prepared soufflé dish. The soufflé may be prepared up to this point, covered, and refrigerated for up to 1$^1$/$_2$ hours.

Bake for 35 to 40 minutes, or until the soufflé is puffy and the top has cracked but the center is still soft. Have the confectioners' sugar ready in a sifter or fine-mesh sieve. Dust the top of the soufflé with the confectioners' sugar and serve immediately with the ice cream and fudge sauce.

# Frango Chocolate Pots de Crème

SERVES 6 ❋ These luscious chocolate custards are a fine choice for entertaining. You can make them a day or two ahead of time, and then take them out of the fridge at the start of the meal, so they're at room temperature when it's time for dessert.

**1 cup milk**

**16 Frango Chocolates (Mint, Dark Mint, Double Chocolate, or Dark Chocolate), chopped, plus more for garnish**

**1 1/2 cups heavy cream**

**6 egg yolks**

**1/3 cup sugar**

**Whipped cream, for serving**

Position a rack in the center of the oven and preheat to 300°F. In a saucepan, bring the milk to a simmer over medium heat. Add the chocolates and stir until melted. Remove from the heat and stir in the cream. Let cool slightly.

In a bowl, whisk together the egg yolks and sugar until well combined but not foamy. Slowly pour the chocolate mixture into the egg yolk mixture, whisking constantly. Strain through a fine-mesh sieve into a pitcher and let stand for 10 minutes.

Divide the mixture evenly among six 3/4-cup ramekins or soufflé dishes. Set the ramekins in a baking pan and place the pan in the oven. Pour hot water into the pan to reach halfway up the sides of the ramekins, and cover the pan with aluminum foil.

Bake for about 1 hour, or until the custards are just set at the edges but still soft in the center. Remove the pan from the oven, take the ramekins out of the water bath, and let the custards cool. Serve warm or at room temperature, or cover and refrigerate for up to 2 days and serve chilled. Top each serving with a dollop of whipped cream and a scattering of Frango Chocolate shavings made with a vegetable peeler.

# Frozen Fun

# Frango Ice Cream Sandwiches

MAKES 8 SANDWICHES ✳ Easy enough to make with kids, but sophisticated enough to be enjoyed by adults, too. Mix and match your favorite flavors of ice cream and Frango Chocolates—you can't go wrong.

**1 pint vanilla ice cream**

**12 Frango Chocolates (Mint, Dark Mint, Double Chocolate, or Dark Chocolate), finely chopped**

**16 chocolate wafer cookies such as Nabisco Famous Chocolate Wafers**

Allow the ice cream to soften at room temperature for 5 minutes. Transfer it to a large bowl and stir it vigorously with a wooden spoon until it is smooth and creamy but still firm. Gently stir in half of the chopped chocolates. Put the remaining chocolates in a shallow bowl.

Working quickly, scoop $1/4$ cup of the ice cream onto the bottom of a cookie. Top with another cookie, bottom down, press gently to spread the ice cream evenly, and roll the edge of the sandwich in the remaining chopped chocolates.

Put the sandwich on a waxed paper–lined baking sheet and immediately place it in the freezer. Repeat with the remaining ingredients, adding each sandwich to the pan as it is made. Freeze the sandwiches for about 1 hour, or until they are solid. Serve immediately, or wrap each sandwich individually in waxed paper and store in the freezer for up to 1 week.

# Mint Stracciatella Ice Cream

MAKES ABOUT 3 PINTS ✳ *Stracciatella* is the Italian version of chocolate chip ice cream, made by swirling melted chocolate into just-frozen ice cream so that the chocolate hardens in little pieces.

**2 cups milk**

**2 cups heavy cream**

**1 cup sugar**

**8 egg yolks**

**1¹/₂ teaspoons vanilla extract**

**12 Frango Dark Mint Chocolates, melted (page 8)**

In a heavy-bottomed saucepan, combine the milk, cream, and ¹/₂ cup of the sugar over medium heat. Bring the mixture to a simmer, whisking frequently. Reduce the heat to low.

In a bowl, whisk together the remaining ¹/₂ cup sugar and the egg yolks. While whisking constantly, slowly pour 1¹/₂ cups of the hot milk mixture into the egg mixture, mixing well. Whisk the egg mixture into the hot milk mixture remaining in the pan and cook over very low heat, stirring constantly with a wooden spoon, for 2 to 4 minutes, or until the mixture forms a custard thick enough to coat the back of the spoon. Do not let the custard come near a boil, or the eggs will curdle. Remove from the heat and stir in the vanilla.

Strain the custard through a fine-mesh sieve into a stainless-steel bowl. Set the bowl over another bowl filled with ice and water, and stir the custard until it is completely chilled (40°F or lower). Alternatively, let the custard cool to room temperature, stirring occasionally, then cover and refrigerate until completely chilled.

Following the manufacturer's directions, freeze the custard in an ice cream maker until it is just firm. With the motor running, drizzle the chocolate into the ice cream in a thin, steady stream. Remove the paddle and break up any large chunks of chocolate with a spoon. Enjoy immediately, or transfer the ice cream to an airtight container and freeze for about 2 hours, or until firm, before serving.

# Frangocino

SERVES 2 ✳ A quick-to-fix frozen mocha drink that tastes like something you'd get at your favorite coffeehouse.

**6 Frango Chocolates (Double Chocolate or Dark Chocolate), plus more for garnish**

**¹/₂ cup milk, heated just to a boil**

**1 teaspoon instant espresso powder**

**1¹/₂ cups ice cubes**

**Whipped cream, for garnish**

Put the chocolates in a blender. Pour the hot milk over the chocolates and add the espresso powder. Place the lid on the blender, cover it with a folded dish towel held in place with your hand, and process on high speed for 1 minute, or until smooth. Add the ice cubes and process on high speed for 1 to 2 minutes, or until smooth.

Divide between 2 tall glasses. Top each glass with a dollop of whipped cream and, using a grater, a scattering of chocolate shavings. Serve immediately.

# Frango Fudge Sauce

MAKES ABOUT 2 1/2 CUPS ✳ Serve this dense sauce warm over ice cream, or enjoy it by the spoonful right from the jar at midnight. Just don't let anyone see you.

- **³/₄ cup heavy cream**
- **¹/₂ cup light corn syrup**
- **30 Frango Chocolates (Mint, Dark Mint, Double Chocolate, or Dark Chocolate)**

In a small, heavy-bottomed saucepan, combine the cream and corn syrup over medium heat and bring just to a boil. Remove from the heat, add the chocolates, and stir until completely melted and smooth. Serve immediately, or let cool, cover, and refrigerate for up to 1 week. Reheat in the microwave or in a heavy-bottomed saucepan over medium-low heat before serving.

**Variation:** If using Frango Double Chocolates or Dark Chocolates, add 1 teaspoon instant espresso powder to the cream and corn syrup before heating.

# Frango Mint Chocolate
# Ice Cream Pie

SERVES 6 TO 8 ✳ If you grew up in Chicago, this time-honored treat from Marshall Field's Walnut Room may well have been your first restaurant dessert. It's a classic graham cracker crust with a homemade ice cream filling that's frozen soft and rushed from the kitchen to arrive at the table just as it's beginning to melt. If you don't have time to make the filling from scratch, you can create a reasonable facsimile by stirring chopped Frango Mint Chocolates into softened store-bought chocolate ice cream.

## CRUST

- 1 1/2 cups graham cracker crumbs (about 18 crackers)
- 6 tablespoons unsalted butter, melted
- 1/4 cup sugar

## FILLING

- 1/2 cup sugar
- 1 1/2 teaspoons cornstarch
- 1/8 teaspoon salt
- 1 cup milk
- 8 Frango Mint Chocolates, finely chopped
- 1 egg, at room temperature
- 1 cup heavy cream
- 1/2 teaspoon vanilla extract

**¹/₂ cup sugar**

**¹/₂ cup toasted, skinned, and coarsely chopped hazelnuts (page 10)**

**Whipped cream, for garnish**

**Crust:** Position a rack in the center of the oven and preheat to 350°F. Butter a 9-inch pie pan. In a food processor, combine the cracker crumbs, butter, and sugar and process until well blended. Transfer to the prepared pie pan and press evenly and firmly into the bottom and sides. Bake for about 8 minutes, or until the crust is beginning to brown. Let cool completely on a rack.

**Filling:** In a heavy-bottomed saucepan, combine the sugar, cornstarch, and salt. Add ¹/₄ cup of the milk and whisk until the cornstarch is dissolved. Add the chocolates and the remaining ³/₄ cup milk and place over medium-low heat. Cook, stirring constantly, for about 4 minutes, or until the mixture just comes to a boil. Remove from the heat.

In a small bowl, whisk the egg until lightly beaten. Gradually add about ¹/₄ cup of the hot chocolate mixture, whisking constantly until blended. Whisk the egg mixture into the saucepan holding the chocolate mixture and place over low heat. Cook, stirring constantly, for about 1 minute, or until the custard is slightly thickened. Do not let the custard come near a boil, or the egg will curdle. Transfer the custard to a bowl and allow to cool completely, stirring occasionally. Stir in the cream and vanilla. Cover and refrigerate for about 2 hours, or until well chilled.

Following the manufacturer's directions, freeze the custard in an ice cream maker until it is frozen but still soft and spreadable. Transfer the ice cream to the cooled crust and smooth the top with a spatula. Cover tightly with plastic wrap and freeze for at least 4 hours, or until very firm. Or cover tightly with plastic wrap and then aluminum foil and store in the freezer for up to 1 week.

continued

**Topping:** Butter a baking sheet. In a small, heavy-bottomed saucepan, combine the sugar and hazelnuts over medium heat. Cook, stirring constantly, for about 5 minutes, or until the sugar starts to dissolve. Reduce the heat to low and continue stirring for about 5 minutes, or until the hazelnuts are well coated and the sugar is caramelized (some of the sugar may remain unmelted). Pour the hazelnut praline onto the prepared baking sheet, spreading it out as much as possible. Let cool completely on a rack.

Using your hands, break the praline into small pieces and transfer to the food processor. Pulse until finely chopped.

Sprinkle the top of the pie with the praline, pressing it in gently to adhere. Garnish with whipped cream and serve immediately.

# Frango Holidays

# Easter Egg Nests

MAKES 6 NESTS ✳ Somewhere between a cookie and a curio, these chocolate nests are fun to make and serve—especially when kids are part of the festivities.

**30 Frango Chocolates (Mint, Dark Mint, Double Chocolate, or Dark Chocolate), melted (page 8)**

**1 cup miniature marshmallows**

**3 cups shoestring potato sticks**

**About 48 jelly beans, small Easter-egg candies, and/or Jordan almonds, for decorating**

In a bowl, combine the chocolate, marshmallows, and potato sticks. Mix well to blend thoroughly.

Line a baking sheet with waxed paper, or with aluminum foil and spray the foil with nonstick spray. Drop the chocolate mixture by scoops onto the prepared baking sheet, forming 6 well-spaced mounds. Using a 1-tablespoon measuring spoon, make an indentation in the center of each mound, forming a "nest." Cover loosely with plastic wrap and refrigerate for about 1 hour, or until set.

Fill the nests with the decorations as desired.

# Halloween Witches' Hats

MAKES 15 "HATS" ❊ With only Frango Chocolates, cereal, and store-bought cookies on hand, you can make these spooky treats at the drop of a ... well, you know.

**15 Frango Dark Chocolates, melted (page 8) and cooled until just tepid**

**2 cups twig-style cereal such as General Mills Fiber One bran cereal**

**15 chocolate wafer cookies such as Nabisco Famous Chocolate Wafers**

**Colored sugar, for garnish**

In a large bowl, combine the melted chocolate and cereal. Toss well to coat the cereal completely.

Arrange the cookies on an aluminum foil–lined baking sheet. Using your hands, mound about 2 tablespoons of the chocolate-cereal mixture on top of each cookie, forming a cone shape and leaving the edges of the cookie exposed. Sprinkle with colored sugar and refrigerate for 1 hour, or until firm. The hats can be stored in an airtight container at room temperature for up to 4 days.

# Candy-Box Christmas Tree

MAKES 1 TREE ❋ This Frango Chocolate–covered tree makes a sparkling edible centerpiece for a holiday table or dessert buffet. Look for Styrofoam cones in crafts and hobby stores.

**1 Styrofoam cone, 12 inches high and 5 inches in diameter at the base**

**Gold wrapping paper**

**Clear adhesive tape**

**About 180 toothpicks**

**About 180 (four 1-pound boxes) Frango Chocolates, in assorted flavors, wrapped or unwrapped, or a combination**

**Floral wire**

**About 25 small round Christmas-tree ornaments**

**1 star ornament**

Wrap the cone in the wrapping paper, and secure the paper with tape. Insert a toothpick into the underside of each Frango Chocolate, being careful not to push it all the way through. Wrap a length of floral wire around the metal base of each ornament, leaving both ends about 1 inch long. Twist the ends together. Starting at the base of the cone, secure the chocolates to the tree by inserting the exposed end of the toothpick through the paper and into the Styrofoam. Secure the ornaments in the same way, pushing the twisted wire into the Styro-foam (it may help to poke a hole first with a toothpick or metal skewer). Continue attaching the chocolates and ornaments to form a pleasing pattern. Top with the star-shaped ornament.

# Frango Ornamints

MAKES 24 ORNAMENTS ❋ Use these candy ornaments to sweeten your own assortment of tree decorations, or put one at each place setting as party favors for guests to take home.

**24 wrapped Frango Chocolates, any flavor**

**24 small sprays decorative red berries or artificial holly berries and/or small candy canes**

**24 (6-inch) lengths holiday ribbon (green, gold, and/or red)**

**24 ornament hooks**

To make each ornament, position a Frango Chocolate on top of a spray of berries. Tie the candy and berries together with a length of ribbon. Slip the ribbon into the base of the hook, and then hang the ornament on the tree.

# Valentine Heartlets

SERVES 4 ✳ Share the love with these elegant chocolate tartlets. If you're pressed for time, you can use store-bought refrigerated sugar cookie dough to make the crust (see variation on page 84). Look for metal heart-shaped tartlet pans about 3 inches across at the widest point and with fluted sides.

CRUST

...............................................................................................................

1 cup all-purpose flour

2 tablespoons sugar

¹/₈ teaspoon salt

5 tablespoons plus 1 teaspoon cold unsalted butter,
    cut into ¹/₂-inch pieces

1 egg yolk, chilled

2 teaspoons ice water

FILLING

...............................................................................................................

5 tablespoons plus 1 teaspoon unsalted butter

12 Frango Chocolates (Double Chocolate or Dark
    Chocolate), finely chopped

¹/₄ cup heavy cream, at room temperature

About 1 pint raspberries

**Crust:** In a bowl, stir together the flour, sugar, and salt. Using a pastry blender or 2 knives, cut the butter into the dry ingredients until the mixture resembles coarse meal. In a small bowl, stir together the egg yolk and ice water. Add to the flour mixture and stir just until the dough comes together. (If the dough seems too dry, sprinkle in additional ice water, 1 teaspoon at a time, until moist enough to hold together.) Shape the dough into a disk, wrap tightly in plastic wrap, and refrigerate for about 1 hour, or until well chilled.

Lightly flour a work surface. Using a floured rolling pin, roll out the dough into an oval about 14 by 8 inches and ¹/₈ to ¹/₄ inch thick.

continued

Using a paring knife, cut the dough into 4 equal pieces. Gently transfer each dough piece to a heart-shaped tartlet pan (see headnote). Press the dough firmly against the bottom and sides, forcing out any air pockets. Trim away the excess dough by pressing it against the fluted rim. Prick the bottom of each crust with fork tines. Cover loosely with plastic wrap and freeze for 30 minutes.

Position a rack in the bottom third of the oven and preheat to 400°F. Line each crust with a piece of aluminum foil and fill with pie weights or dried beans. Bake for 10 minutes. Remove the weights and foil and continue to bake for about 10 minutes, or until uniformly golden. Let cool completely in the pans on a rack.

**Filling:** In a small saucepan, melt the butter over low heat. Remove from the heat, add the chocolates, and let stand for 1 minute. Whisk until smooth. Whisk in the cream until well blended.

Invert the tartlet pans to remove the cooled pastry shells. Place the shells upright on a platter. Pour the filling into the shells, dividing it evenly. Arrange the raspberries, standing them upright, in a ring around the edge of each tartlet. Cover with plastic wrap and refrigerate for 4 hours, or until the filling is firm. The tartlets can be stored in the refrigerator for up to 1 day. Bring to room temperature before serving.

**Variation:** To make the tartlet shells with store-bought refrigerated sugar cookie dough, press the dough directly into the pans, covering the bottom and pushing it up the sides. It should be about 1/4 inch thick. Bake until golden brown and crisp (a few minutes longer than the package directions indicate for cookies). Remove from the oven, let cool slightly, and pat down the warm dough with your fingertips, flattening it against the bottom and sides of the pans. Let cool completely, unmold, and proceed as directed.

# Resources

Look for Frango Chocolates, special seasonal items, and other Frango products at your local Macy's store.

To order by phone, call Macy's Frango hotline at 1-800-5FRANGO (1-800-537-2646).

To purchase select Frango products online, visit www.macys.com.

When in Chicago, visit the Frango Café on the seventh floor of Macy's at 111 North State Street.

**Note:** As Frango Chocolates evolved during the twentieth century, two recipes emerged: those sold by Marshall Field's in rectangular boxes and those most recently sold at The Bon Marché and Bon-Macy's stores in the Pacific Northwest in hexagonal boxes. Today, both recipes are part of the Macy's family. The Frango recipe sold in rectangular boxes is the predominant brand and is available at Macy's nationwide. The chocolates sold in the hexagonal box are only available at Macy's stores in the Pacific Northwest. The recipes in this cookbook have been tested using the Frango Chocolates sold in the rectangular box. You may experience varied results if you use other products.

# Index

## Acknowledgments

The Book Kitchen thanks Macy's team members Warren Wolfe, Elizabeth Brown, Tim Scott, Debbie Thompson, Sara Lynn Nash, and Kelly Lainsbury for their help in producing this book. We would also like to thank Gale Gand, Tamsen and Marion Salvador, Dave Hambright, and Brown Caruso Schneider for their support and sweet ideas.

ISBN 0-9779890-3-8
First printing, 2007
Printed and bound in China by Overseas Printing Corporation
10 9 8 7 6 5 4 3 2 1

Conceived and produced by The Book Kitchen, San Francisco, CA, www.bookkitchen.com, for Macy's North.

Design Director: **Catherine Jacobes**
Editorial Director: **Steve Siegelman**
Photography: **Maren Caruso**
Photography Assistance: **Faiza Ali** and **Scott Mansfield**
Food Stylists: **George Dolese** and **Elisabet der Nederlanden**
Prop Stylist: **Emma Star Jensen**
Digital Imaging: **Lauren Burke**
Copyeditor: **Sharon Silva**
Proofreader: **Rebecca Pepper**
Indexer: **Ken DellaPenta**